BEST WISHES HERE!

MISSISSIPPI BABY
THE MAGNOLIA STATE BABY'S BOOK OF FIRSTS

Written & Illustrated by Allison Dugas Behan

To my girls, Brennan & Claire

The word "Pelican" and the depiction of a pelican are trademarks of Arcadia Publishing Company Inc. and are registered in the U.S. Patent and Trademark Office.

ISBN: 978-1-4556-2630-4

Printed in Korea
Published by Pelican Publishing
New Orleans, LA
www.pelicanpub.com

WELCOME

NAME

BIRTHDAY

FIRST PICTURE

MY FAMILY TREE

FOOTPRINTS

HANDPRINTS

MY FAMILY

ALL THE DETAILS

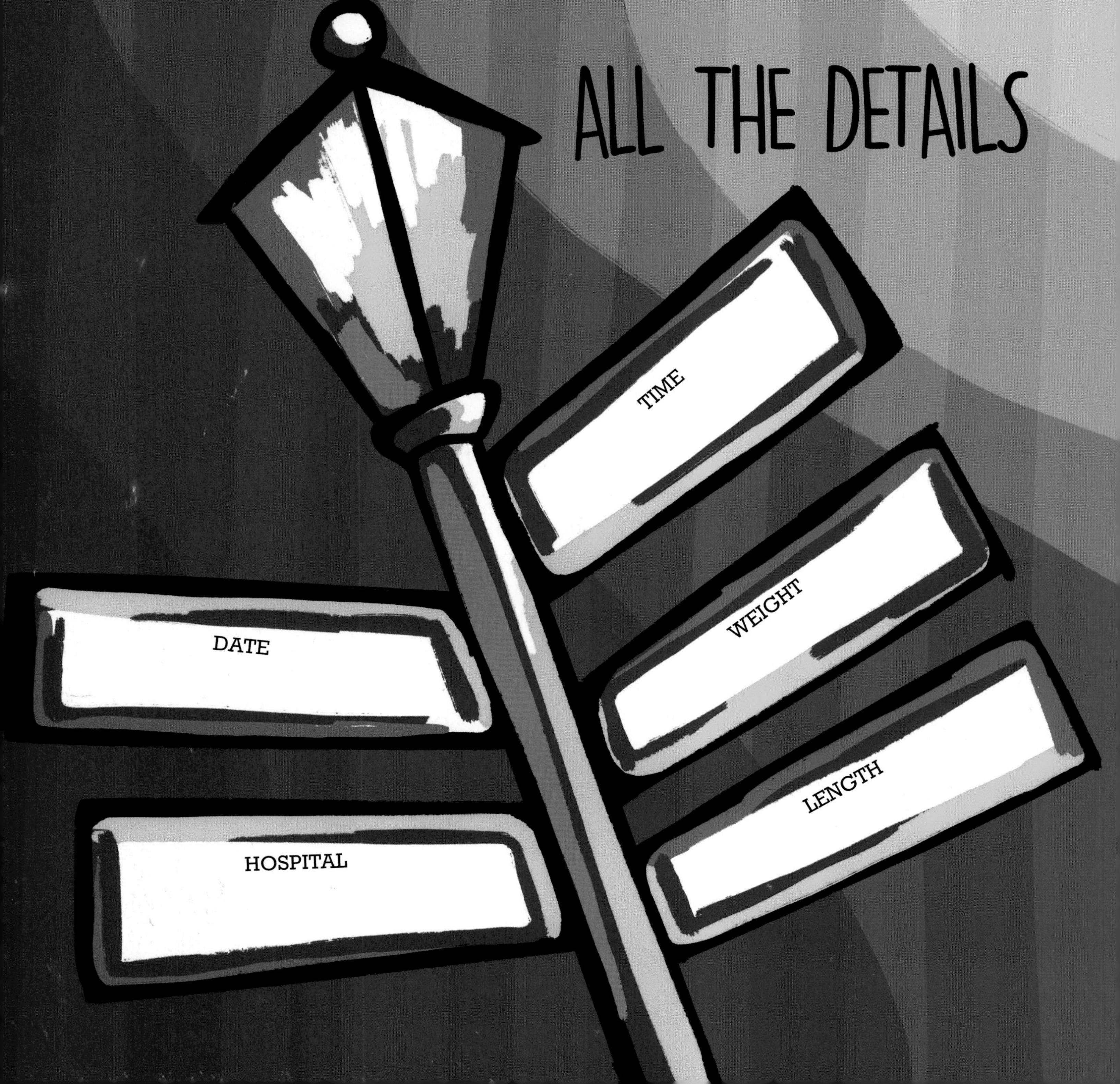

HOME SWEET HOME

MY FIRST ADDRESS

1 MONTH

MILESTONES & FAVORITES

2 MONTHS

MILESTONES & FAVORITES

1 MONTH PICTURE

2 MONTHS PICTURE

3
MONTHS

MILESTONES & FAVORITES

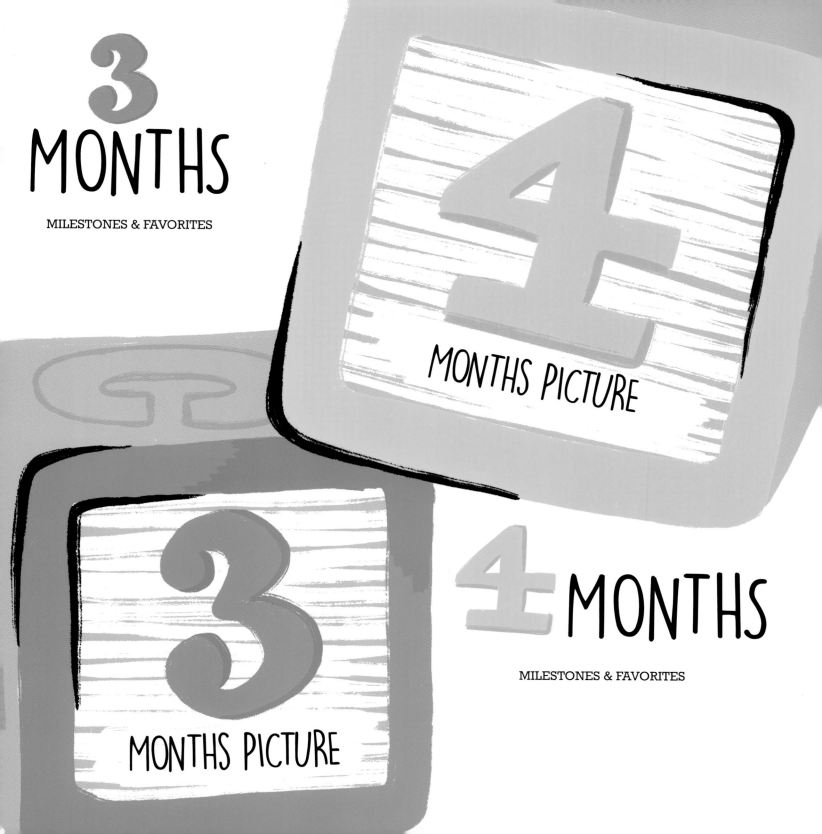

MONTHS PICTURE

MONTHS PICTURE

4
MONTHS

MILESTONES & FAVORITES

5

MONTHS PICTURE

6
MONTHS

MILESTONES & FAVORITES

5 MONTHS

MILESTONES & FAVORITES

6

MONTHS PICTURE

7

MONTHS PICTURE

7 MONTHS

MILESTONES & FAVORITES

8 MONTHS

MILESTONES & FAVORITES

8

MONTHS PICTURE

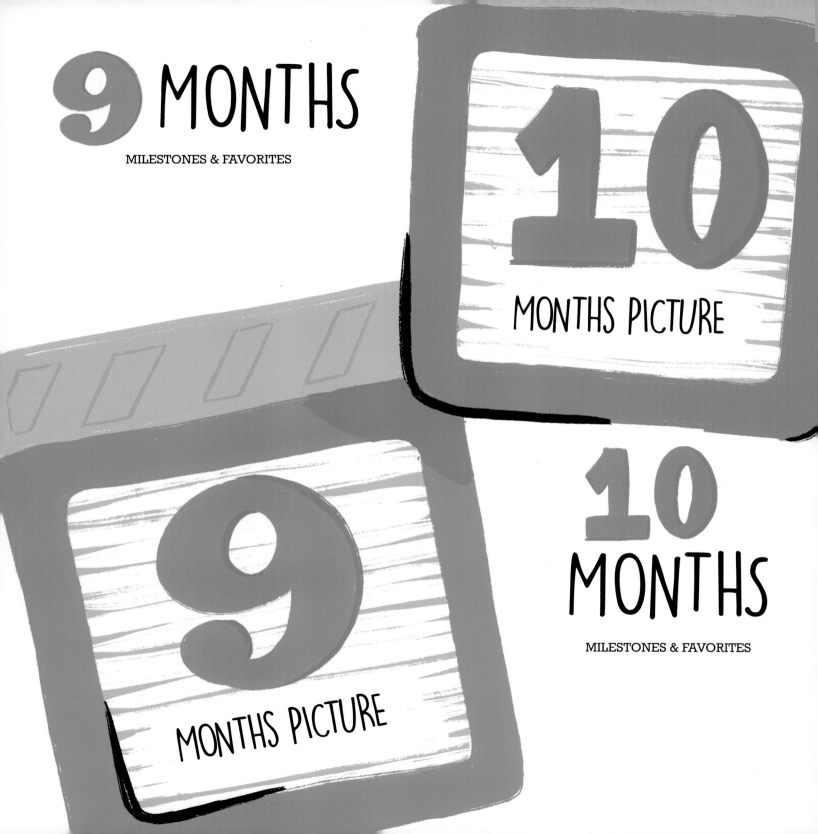

11
MONTHS
MILESTONES & FAVORITES

12
MONTHS PICTURE

11
MONTHS PICTURE

12
MONTHS
MILESTONES & FAVORITES

PARTY THEME

PARTY LOCATION

SPECIAL GUESTS

FAVORITE GIFTS

1ST BIRTHDAY

2ND BIRTHDAY

PARTY THEME

SPECIAL GUESTS

PARTY LOCATION

FAVORITE GIFTS

YUMMY FOOD!

FIRST FRIED
CHICKEN

MY REACTION

WHO TOOK ME

RESTAURANT

DATE

FIRST BBQ

DATE

WHO MADE IT

MY FAVORITE TYPE OF BBQ

FIRST BISCUITS AND GRAVY

DATE   WHO MADE 'EM   MY REACTION

FIRST SNOBALL

DATE

FLAVOR

STAND

FIRST BLACK BOTTOM PIE

DATE

BAKERY

FIRST MISSISSIPPI MUD PIE

DATE   BAKERY   MY REACTION

FIRST CRAWFISH

DATE

PLACE

MY REACTION

FIRST
SHRIMP

DATE

PLACE

FIRST CATFISH

DATE

PLACE

FIRST ACTIVITIES

AND EVENTS!

FIRST FOOTBALL GAME

DATE

PLACE

TEAMS

FINAL SCORE

FIRST BASKETBALL GAME

DATE

PLACE

TEAMS

FINAL SCORE

FIRST PARADE

DATE

FAVORITE CATCH

PARADE

FAVORITE FLOAT

FIRST FESTIVAL

DATE

FESTIVAL NAME

WHO WENT WITH ME

WHAT I ENJOYED

FIRST
ZOO TRIP

DATE

ZOO NAME

WHO WENT WITH ME

FAVORITE ANIMAL

FIRST
AQUARIUM TRIP

DATE

AQUARIUM NAME

WHO WENT WITH ME

FAVORITE ANIMAL

FIRST MUSEUM

DATE

MUSEUM NAME

FAVORITE EXHIBIT

PEOPLE WITH ME

FIRST VISIT TO JACKSON

DATE

PLACES I EXPLORED

FAVORITE SIGHTS

PEOPLE WITH ME

FIRST FISHING TRIP

DATE

WHO TOOK ME

LOCATION

WHAT I CAUGHT

FIRST VISIT TO THE NATCHEZ TRACE

DATE

AREA

PEOPLE WITH ME

FAVORITE SIGHTS

FIRST BOAT RIDE

DATE

NAME OF BOAT

FAVORITE SIGHTS

PEOPLE WITH ME

FIRST HOLIDAYS

 EASTER

DATE

FAVORITE TREAT

WHERE I CELEBRATED

FAMILY WITH ME

 THANKGIVING

DATE

FAVORITE FOOD

WHERE I CELEBRATED

FAMILY WITH ME

  4TH OF JULY

DATE

FAVORITE TREAT

WHERE I CELEBRATED

FAMILY WITH ME

 CHRISTMAS

DATE

FAVORITE GIFT

WHERE I CELEBRATED

FAMILY WITH ME

 HALLOWEEN

DATE

FAVORITE TREAT

TRICK-OR-TREAT SPOT

MY COSTUME

 NEW YEAR'S

DATE

HOW I CELEBRATED

WHERE I CELEBRATED

FAMILY WITH ME

ALL THE LITTLE EXTRAS

FIRST SMILE

DATE

FIRST LAUGH

DATE

FIRST ROLL OVER

DATE

FIRST CRAWL

DATE

FIRST TIME SITTING UP

DATE

FIRST STEPS

DATE

FIRST TIME I WALKED

DATE

FIRST WORD

DATE

FAVORITE SONG

FAVORITE FOOD

FAVORITE TV SHOW

FAVORITE TOY